This Woman Alphabetical

THIS WOMAN

ALPHABETICAL

poems by

LAURA FARINA

Pedlar Press | Toronto

ACKNOWLEDGEMENTS
The publisher wishes to thank the Canada Council for the Arts
and the Ontario Arts Council for their generous support of our
publishing program.

LIBRARY AND ARCHIVES CANADA CATALOGUING
IN PUBLICATION

Farina, Laura, 1980-
      This woman alphabetical / Laura Farina.
Poems.
ISBN 1-897141-04-1
      I. Title.
PS8611.A755T48 2005   C811'.6   C2005-901231-5

First Edition

COVER ART Laura Fetterley, 2004

DESIGN Zab Design & Typography, Winnipeg

Printed in Canada

THE CANADA COUNCIL | LE CONSEIL DES ARTS
FOR THE ARTS | DU CANADA
SINCE 1957 | DEPUIS 1957

ONTARIO ARTS COUNCIL
CONSEIL DES ARTS DE L'ONTARIO

For Heather

TABLE OF CONTENTS

bugs

In summer I am nowhere bug.
Gnat or dragonfly has no internal compass.
I see the wind.
I hear the wind.
I smell the wind.
I taste the wind. Tastes like tuna.
When I touch you gently
do you know what I mean?

I taste your beauty
but I do not sigh.

You could say
John Wayne the mosquito
on his steed of blood
rides off into this Ontario.

The thing is how big I am,
filling two saddles,
two lawn chairs.
I can't fit on any escalators.

You still understand, don't you?

You say this must
follow that
and can I make this woman alphabetical?

On this day raccoons
and honkytonk piano.

Did your sunburnt nose notice
that R should follow H?

Alphabetically speaking, of course.

When the road ahead starts bending,
don't worry
as long as you can smell me
you're still going
the right way.

Ten. Ten. Ten.

The ten wasps of earnestness,
the ones we fled in childhood.
That childhood that was
long and hard like beetle backs.

We drew our pistols in the kitchen.
We rode our horses down the basement stairs.
Ask Tiger-Toes what stories she had that night.
She will write
a fight that broke out
when your lasso got tangled.
She will write how she said
cockroaches, and you didn't believe her.

I think in the buzzing noise
of hair growing
or the chattering
teeth of whisky
pouring into glass.
Your scraped knees
from falling off that high horse.

A rainstorm is why
the bread didn't rise
and I think that is what
John Wayne meant by
"la vie en rose."

Even as the mosquitoes of August
stop their diplomatic relations
I am cactus
        and nowhere
                at once.

great pan is dead

A pie maker
is a keeper of secrets.

Juice flesh
under flakes
like the snowy months
when neighbours tie scarves
and grow fatter.

A circle eats its own tail
as summer bakes
under a pie plate moon.

This is seasons of forgetfulness.

So hard to think sweat
with goosebumped arms.
So hard to think forest
when only knife branches
and nowhere sky remain.

A pie maker
whispers the promise
of rising to blackbirds
and they have marbles in their stomachs.
Cat's eyes peering out
the windpipe of a bird.

Difficult to fly while digesting clocks.

In spring we hear
Pan is dead
and there is
a new cat king.

He cuts through
pale pie maker palms
and blood pours out
like gravy.

my true-life adventures with aquaboy

Today at the Y
I met my very own Aquaboy —
webbed-foot wonder
with a whisk. Maker of
omelettes that cause my mouth
to water,
spill out onto the kitchen floor.
I watch the tiles become
slippery — soon I can no
longer see my dog.

Aquaboy of the slime skin
swimming through
my saliva to
the back door
just in time.
My dog turning blue.

As we wait
for the kitchen
to drain
we walk out in the park —
feed the ducks because
it's hard to tell
exactly which one is
his mother and
besides it's good to
be charitable to all
living things.

He kisses me then —
pours himself
into my mouth.

As his flippered hand
lodges itself
in my water-tangled hair, I realize
that it will never work
between us. Him, too
much a creature of the deep
and my lung capacity is poor.

I walk him to the edge of the lake.
The tears that run down his face are
tiny drops of home.
I run my hand across his gills
and then like so many fish
I throw him back.

ten ways of looking, at me

1.
A quarter held between forefinger
and thumb
is the moon.
I could howl at it
or feed it to a telephone
and howl at your answering machine.

2.
I am not that sort of girl
I like that sort of girl
but I am not her.

3.
The pigeons on my street
pose questions about cruelty.
If one has the desire to kick
but does not
is that righteousness?

4.
It is spring.
A crocus blooms
then croaks.
An inevitably muddy season.

5.
On Wednesday I fall in love
with the word passion.
We have a distant relationship.
He refuses to touch me.

6.
Alone again
at midnight
I think silence
must be a liquid
and find myself thirsty.

7.
I rarely think about death
but often about headaches.
They could be similar.
Like woodpeckers
in jam jars.

8.
I like armchairs.

9.
I saw a man
who looked like you
at the grocery store.
And later
another man who
looked like you
cut in front of me
at the cinema.
Possibly the same man?

10.
Last night
I thought very hard
about calling you —
but chose instead to sleep.

borrowed stories

I could be either
very rich or very married
but I could not be either with you.

So much temporary about us
is a pair of
missing sunglasses
left almost accidentally
in Lebanon, Ohio
and only remembered
as the car pointed home.

Sometimes my daydreams
about you
are images of Kerouac.
You thumb your way
across America
like a terrible cactus.

I want to thank you
for the bear claw
which you gave me
and which I use
to ward off the
uncertainty of
airplanes, cars, trains, buses.

Sometimes I think
the only reason I am not forgotten
in the restroom
in a gas station
in Lebanon, Ohio
is your instinctive hand.

in praise of simplicity

Today I praise only what is simple.
A white bowl full of white milk.
The weight of a hand full of river stones.
Feet and the creak of hardwood floors.
The last of this summer's ripe tomatoes.

Today I praise only what is simple.
A spill falling like white silk.
The weight of silence broken by the phone.
Suitcase and a slamming door.
An empty room and an open window.

private tyson in the field

clip clop clip
go private tyson's boots

boots say to ground
don't mess with me

boots say
stomp say
get your ass-kickings here say
highways and license plates
and smog and billboards
and nervous twitches
and all those late library books
can get the fuck out of town

she polishes them
every morning
and they're black
with rubber soles

black boots
punching ground
are fists with knuckles
pointing out.

picnicking, in the park

Amid tomatoes red as
nipples resting in
mouths wanting more
I picnic with my sexually adventurous
friends in the park.

I cannot tell if
when they ask me to pass the iced tea
they mean simply reaching
or cool liquid sliding
like a hand under the
cotton of my t-shirt.

I blush tomato.
Oh shit I'm blushing nipple,
blushing with the pulled back
lips of something lower.

When I picnic with
my sexually adventurous
friends in the park
sandwiches could be
code for underwear and
I know that theirs are pink or leopard spot
and mine are only the
white kind you buy
in a bag at Zellers.

Oh please let them not
insist that we play capture
the flag — fly our undies
secretly on sticks in the bush.

Fuck, no. Don't mention bush.
Don't mention fuck.
Don't make masturbatory movements
along the neck of the iced tea bottle.

Try not to think like
a cucumber
or the lemon jelly
at the centre of a doughnut.

Try to think like
a water beetle
skimming the top of a lake.

Thoughts smooth
and wet
and nothing at all
like semen.

and when you meet me at my border

And this more human love will consist in this...that two solitudes protect and border and salute each other.
— RAINER MARIA RILKE

And when you meet me at my border we will not embrace but nod in recognition and fall into step with each other.

And when you meet me at my border I will be hungry and you will be hungry but we will not eat.

And when you meet me at my border I will say my mother had many lovers but she was always faithful.

And when you meet me at my border the words will be thinking and breathing and scared.

And when you meet me at my border — revolving doors.

And when you meet me at my border I will feel your silence like fish passing.

And when you meet me at my border what is round in me will look out and recognize the shape of what is round in you.

And when you meet me at my border the border will stay and you will stay and there will be nothing wrong with that.

the last of the casey poems

Losing the mind of a dog
like waking up beside a bear.
I become aware
of the teeth in her.

Last Wednesday we came home
to find her frantic —
circling the bathroom floor —
the refusal of a caged animal
in her eyes.

My father calls on
his cellphone driving
home along Highway 7.
Her empty collar fills
the seat beside him.

That moment when
you hold what you
have already let go.
The vet poisoned her vein.
My father held fur, bones, breath
until everything about her
stopped.

On the phone
his voice is the empty sound
a highway makes.
It is silent in the car.
He has not turned on the radio.

the sun and jeremy sit on a hill

There is a soft
calling like a rounded e.
An overheard conversation
remembered in song.

I wonder if he even sees
where the sun
is dipping to read
over his shoulder.

He has aphids in his mouth.
He wrestles them with a
silent tongue
and they have almost
stopped thrashing.

Tomorrow he will be boy.
Tonight he is the sun's scribe.
He sits on the hill writing
a recipe for flight.

the juice poems

1. You Can't Spell Juice Without J.C.

show me your juices oh bible-reading man
your apple plum hibiscus root fruit
tough tongues speak like gushing
say mango like praying
st. juicous' passion on the mount
said with birds in his mouth
when moses parted the juice and led his people to
a promised puree
there were liquid vitamins
and they drank deep
of god.

2. Juice and German Reunification

the fall of the wall
happened like this —

a woman with apple juice
in a plastic cup.

with mittened hands
and frozen tongue
she sips the slip
of cement to ground

she drinks up all the juice
then drinks up all the wall
turns and walks boldly
towards the camera men

who have already
arrived on the scene.

3. Recurring Nightmares

i have something to say
but when i open
my mouth
juice pours out
and they feed at me
like a trough.

4. Thirst

the arctic explorer
after months in the cold
could not remember the taste
of his wife's nipple

sat back and remembered
sweet apple cider
the way his taste buds
stung with it.

kept thinking
why juice and not her?

his crew knew
his mind was gone
when they woke
to find him
licking.

5. A Doctoral Thesis On Juice In 18th Century
   Literature

she drinks juice
from a teacup
while all around her
england reacquaints
itself with nature.

she looks out her window
and thinks —
there are daffodils
in those fields
god created them and they
are part of god
and england is part
of god
and juice is part of god.

she sips it daintly
and feels it
grow in her stomach
like a tree.

the symbolism
of it all.

aunt betty

My Aunt Betty is a bit like a fire hydrant.
Her knees are bolts that hold her upright
and she sprays out all my fires.

She needs a magnifying glass to see her cross-stitch.
She hears every time I take the Lord's name in vain.
She eats roast chicken every Sunday night.
She can smell pop cans open before lunch.
She pets my dog behind the ears.
She sees a mouse sour on the mantel.

My Wonder Woman in Lindsay, Ontario.

My Aunt Betty is not at all like a fire hydrant.
She has curves and she ruffles my hair as she passes.

I shouldn't be here.

Oh my shattered nerves and heavens to Betsy
when my Aunt Betty and Uncle Bill
swing dance to 40s music in the afternoons.

The reason I miss her is because
I have bungee chords attached to my ankles.

She says,
"You should write down all you remember,
before you are old like I am."
She says,
"If you freeze spaghetti sauce you
can use it whenever."

I like to watch
the green elbow of her afternoon,

the way it stretches lazy
as a young boy in the sun.

My Aunt Betty waxes the sky
until it sparkles and then turns
her attention to the kitchen floor.

"You scamp!" she calls me when I tease her
but "Laura" when I am in my grey and serious moods.

I will have her front row centre.
I will read straight to her.
I will find a way to repay her.
I will mimic her ant-like hands.

She makes sermons to the sandbox fleas
that make them sit up
and stop biting.

"Combien de pomme de terre," she says.
She never took French immersion.

Her needle says,
I am as busy as your Aunt Betty's fingers
and it curls through my Aunt Betty's cross-stitch
that is for a wedding present
sometime in the future.

She says,
"It's good to plan ahead."

Red, metal with water pressure
held below the surface.

emily carr; from what i've seen

There was a totem pole once
in a museum downtown
wind-beaten wood
brown and wrinkled
    like the faces
    of my retired grandparents
    after a winter in Florida.
Hooked noses, glaring eyes
and four of us could just
touch fingers
when we reached our arms around.

There was a pine tree
in my backyard
dry green branches leaning left
and I have seen fog
almost embraceable.

There was the sea
one summer in Prince Edward Island.
After a swim
my tongue circling my lips
tasted salt
but this was not the salt
of dinner tables. This was salt.
Grey and wild.

i have longed to move away

Our town is small
like playing to
a room full of friends.
Its sidewalks hold us
at the knees.
Bending impossible,
we learn to stand.

Tomorrow when we wake our stories
will have ripened. Their juices
will flow south and acquire accents.

Only our smiles
will be more permanent.

Logic states
there must be
roads out of the forest.
There were roads in.

I find a crumbling map
in the glove compartment
of a rusted out car.

A midnight dip.
Our white potato bodies
in dark water.

I swim back to you
with stamps in my hand
saying, this is where
we've never been.

a little poem about the heinlich manoeuvre

Think of the small stops on a journey.
Think of a gas station at 2 a.m.
Think Miles.

Miles is a man
who smells of
rotting mushrooms
but it is just the
stench of the law
about him.
It sticks to him
through his days
like a gold star
or a badge.

I watch him through binoculars.
He does not jaywalk.

Miles in a white room.
This is symbolic
of his soul
and also of
new beginnings.

Think blank page
Think first snowfall.

A man
who may or may not
own a truck
greets him.
His bicep says
that he loves mom.

His breath says that
he loves bourbon.
He wears a shirt like
interlocking brick
and carries a phallic chainsaw
though this might be overcompensating.

Miles does not catch this —
unobservant as
good people can be.

Think Mother Teresa blindfolded.
Think St. Francis of Assisi with an eye patch.

The man's arms around
Miles, squeezing.
Out pops good.
It bounces twice.

Miles finds he wants
to get into
his saviour's pants.

I pick up the good and swallow it whole.

Think Tylenol.
Think frog.

the morning of your funeral

The morning of your funeral
I woke five hours away
from all churches.
I left my bed
and walked in the opposite direction
of all holes, all candles, all handkerchiefs.

You were a woman
of electric coleslaws,
you had a wild boar's head
mounted on your wall
beside your rifle.
I do not love these things about you
but think of your shoreline as pebbled and dangerous.

One orange night
you dumped a plastic bag
of pennies onto our kitchen table
and told us we could keep
whatever we rolled into brown paper.

Our hands smelled of copper
and everywhere
glinting brown.

The morning of your funeral
I watched a parking lot
fill, then empty —
a raining down of money
into leaving hands.

two tourists kissing

Who invented the human heart, I wonder? Tell me,
and then show me the place where he was hanged.
— LAWRENCE DURRELL

1.
On the subway platform
I glance back
like lovers parting
at a man on a stretcher
sucking oxygen
from a mask.

2.
I walk to you
without stopping
except for once
when a firetruck
crosses my path.

3.
The sound of a distant siren
breaks the silence like a kiss.

4.
On Yonge St.
you hold my hand.
We could be any couple
watching the ambulance pass.

5.
I say — how strange
the number of emergency
vehicles we've seen since
we got here.
You say — six.

It has the weight of a stone falling.

6.
On Saturday you leave.
One street over
the house on the corner
starts burning.

morning, at blair's

Today I woke early
white light of morning
and the shadows
on your carpet
like the rungs of a ladder.

I woke and you
already had on your hat
and coat.
Knapsack full.
You were lacing your boots.

I said —
Where are you going
with only warmth
and shoelaces?

You said —
It's already 8.
I have to go.
Sleep a little longer.

The white light of morning.
The shadows on the carpet.
My eyelids heavy.

I thought of ladders
and the already trampled snow.
It seemed so epic
and your knapsack was full.

I said —
The sun is like a ladder this morning.
You will never come home.

You kissed me then
from under your hat and said —
You're silly in the morning.
I'll be home at 3.
Get some sleep.

And in the white light of 8 o'clock
and the shadows on the carpet
I rolled away from your coat and slept.

madonna on the ferris wheel

The county fair
bulldozes its way
through August.

At the gate I hand over
all my money and
get on the Ferris wheel.
I sit down beside Madonna.
She is designer jeans
stuck to seat with bubble gum.

When the ride starts
I think I hear
her face creak.

And she is always looking
like fun mirrors,
looking like
how at the fish pond
everyone gets a prize.

Ferris wheel whips
like ice cream
and Madonna is flying
so fast her eyelashes fall off.

She spreads her arms
impossibly wide and
screams the world.

I look down and see
children
making forgettable connections
at the petting zoo.
Their hands on the warm backs
of llamas.

neighbourhood

Our neighbourhood is
brick houses left out
to pasture.

At night
even the dogs of our street,
silent thin creatures,
sit on the steps of the laundromat
and ask passersby for cigarettes.

It is not enough to say
that we have only planted
the most fragrant herbs in our garden,
that the wine we drink
on the porch is always cold,
that we shut our ears
to the arguments, the protest calls,
that the taste of our conversation
lingers in the air like summer.

Last night you told me
that we would have to
start locking the door.

Our house is owned
by Louis Albert Taylor,
born in Brighton, Ontario,
who works in advertising,
who is my uncle.

No, wait. Also,

Our house is owned
by Karen Elizabeth MacQuarrie
who is a teacher and an editor,
who is my aunt.

I wish the drunks would stop
leaving garbage on my lawn.

Today the hippies next door
are building a shed out back.
A broken bicycle holds up one wall
or maybe it is held up
by visions of a brighter future.
We lend them our stepladder.

In our neighbourhood
the cats sneak past
at the door
when our arms are occupied
with groceries.
Shedding the white fur
of belonging
all over our pillowcases.

On hot days
the sweet smell
of the neighbourhood
compost heap.

From my position
midway up the sky
I call to the people
heading into the convenience store.

I say – "Don't forget milk!"
I say – "There's a special on cat food."

From up here
I will see the men
returning from the Quaker Oats plant.
I will see the police car round the corner
one more time.
I will see you come home.

Purple lateness paints your sky.

I wait midway up the horizon
for your bus to pull up beside me
and for you to get off
and walk me downwards home.

Our neighbourhood has
graffitied stop signs
that read —
Stop
War
Arrete
La Guerre.

We walk slowly around them
as we would a picket line.

On our porch
we wait for the front door
to welcome us.
It remains locked.

Everywhere our neighbourhood waits

Green
        solemn
                slow.

ACKNOWLEDGEMENTS

I would like to thank Beth Follett for being a
keen editor, a patient friend, a fine publisher
and a first-rate human being.

Blair Anderson, Chris Gully, Jamila-Khanom
Allidina, Jessie Park-Wheeler, Nathan
Rambukkana, Brooke Phillips and Zach Gaviller
provided editorial comments that were crucial in
the shaping of these poems.

Robin Kent deserves more recognition than I
can give for being my confidante, champion,
advisor and best friend for the past 11 years.

Michael Fitzpatrick is a remarkable creative writ-
ing teacher, who gave me all the right books at
all the right times.

I would like to thank Janet and Chummer
Farina for their guidance and support.

For safe refuge, I am indebted to Karen, Louis
and Dylan Taylor, The JBI Crew, Canterbury
High School and Centauri Summer Arts Camp.

Glenn Clifton – thank you.

.

LAURA FARINA is a poet who lives in Ottawa.
She teaches creative writing to young people
and is one of the editors of *Under The Poet Tree:
A Centauri Anthology* (Pedlar Press, 2004).